iCA
Create Change

ICAN_ALWAYS WELLNESS JOURNAL

Personal Details

This Journal Belongs To:

Date Started:

Date Completed:

Emergency Contact:

Name

Contact

How To Use

"By Failing to prepare, you are preparing to fail."
– Benjamin Franklin.

- Use the introduction section to identify what your long-term (Year wellness goal is. Highlighting what you aim to achieve.)

- Break this into year micro goals monthly, weekly and daily.
For example. Mediate 5 mins daily. Reflect every Friday, Self-care weekend at the end of each month.

- Put a minimum of three items in each.

- Continue to refer back to these tasks and try be consistent with at-least one. Especially on a challenging day.

- As you go through the journal. Be sure to set realistic daily goals in the morning and then spend time in the evening to reflect on how the day was. This helps reduce anxiety and helps you be more aware of your here and now.

- Find 5 things you are grateful for everyday.

- Write at-least a page on how your day was and what you're most looking forward to for the next day.

Let's Get Started!

Be Commited, Be Consistent, Be Resilient! You'll Do Great!!!

#CREATECHANGE

Introduction: Setting the Foundation

Be Intentional about what you are going to achieve. The habits you aim to implement. Visualise who you will become because you're almost there.

LONG TERM WELLNESS GOALS

DAILY WELLNESS TASKS

WEEKLY WELLNESS TASKS

MONTHLY WELLNESS TASKS

Date:
_____

ONE THING TO ACHIEVE TODAY

AFFIRMATIONS FOR THE DAY

MORNING

TODAY'S PERSONAL GOALS

☐ PERSONALLY _____

☐ RELATIONALLY _____

☐ PROFESSIONALLY _____

NOTES:

EVENING

TODAY I AM THANKFUL FOR...

1 _____
2 _____
3 _____
4 _____
5 _____

DEAR JOURNAL...   *Journal Pages*

How was your day? The highlights and how do you feel?

What does tomorrow look like for you? How can you make tomorrow a better day?

_____
_____
_____
_____
_____
_____
_____
_____
_____
_____
_____
_____
_____
_____
_____
_____
_____
_____

Date:
_____

ONE THING TO ACHIEVE TODAY

MORNING

AFFIRMATIONS FOR THE DAY

TODAY'S PERSONAL GOALS

☐ PERSONALLY _____

☐ RELATIONALLY _____

☐ PROFESSIONALLY _____

NOTES:

EVENING

1 _____

2 _____

3 _____

4 _____

5 _____

DEAR JOURNAL...   *Journal Pages*

How was your day? The highlights and how do you feel?

What does tomorrow look like for you? How can you make tomorrow a better day?

_____
_____
_____
_____
_____
_____
_____
_____
_____
_____
_____
_____
_____
_____
_____
_____
_____
_____
_____
_____
_____
_____

Date:

ONE THING TO ACHIEVE TODAY

MORNING

AFFIRMATIONS FOR THE DAY

TODAY'S PERSONAL GOALS

PERSONALLY _____

RELATIONALLY _____

PROFESSIONALLY _____

NOTES:

EVENING

TODAY I AM THANKFUL FOR...

1. _____
2. _____
3. _____
4. _____
5. _____

DEAR JOURNAL...

Journal Pages

How was your day? The highlights and how do you feel?
What does tomorrow look like for you? How can you make tomorrow a better day?

_____
_____
_____
_____
_____
_____
_____
_____
_____
_____
_____
_____
_____
_____
_____
_____
_____
_____
_____

Date:

ONE THING TO ACHIEVE TODAY

MORNING

AFFIRMATIONS FOR THE DAY

TODAY'S PERSONAL GOALS

PERSONALLY _____

RELATIONALLY _____

PROFESSIONALLY _____

NOTES:

EVENING

TODAY I AM THANKFUL FOR...

1. _____
2. _____
3. _____
4. _____
5. _____

DEAR JOURNAL...

Journal Pages

How was your day? The highlights and how do you feel?
What does tomorrow look like for you? How can you make tomorrow a better day?

_____
_____
_____
_____
_____
_____
_____
_____
_____
_____
_____
_____
_____
_____
_____
_____
_____
_____
_____
_____
_____

Date:

ONE THING TO ACHIEVE TODAY

MORNING

AFFIRMATIONS FOR THE DAY

TODAY'S PERSONAL GOALS

PERSONALLY _____

RELATIONALLY _____

PROFESSIONALLY _____

NOTES:

EVENING

1 _____
2 _____
3 _____
4 _____
5 _____

DEAR JOURNAL...   *Journal Pages*

How was your day? The highlights and how do you feel?
What does tomorrow look like for you? How can you make tomorrow a better day?

_____
_____
_____
_____
_____
_____
_____
_____
_____
_____
_____
_____
_____
_____
_____
_____
_____
_____
_____

Date:

ONE THING TO ACHIEVE TODAY

MORNING

AFFIRMATIONS FOR THE DAY

TODAY'S PERSONAL GOALS

PERSONALLY _____

RELATIONALLY _____

PROFESSIONALLY _____

NOTES:

EVENING

1 _____

2 _____

3 _____

4 _____

5 _____

DEAR JOURNAL...   *Journal Pages*

How was your day? The highlights and how do you feel?

What does tomorrow look like for you? How can you make tomorrow a better day?

_____
_____
_____
_____
_____
_____
_____
_____
_____
_____
_____
_____
_____
_____
_____
_____
_____
_____
_____
_____
_____
_____

Date:

ONE THING TO ACHIEVE TODAY

MORNING

AFFIRMATIONS FOR THE DAY

TODAY'S PERSONAL GOALS

PERSONALLY _____

RELATIONALLY _____

PROFESSIONALLY _____

NOTES:

EVENING

1. _____
2. _____
3. _____
4. _____
5. _____

DEAR JOURNAL...

Journal Pages

How was your day? The highlights and how do you feel?

What does tomorrow look like for you? How can you make tomorrow a better day?

_____
_____
_____
_____
_____
_____
_____
_____
_____
_____
_____
_____
_____
_____
_____
_____
_____
_____
_____

Date:

ONE THING TO ACHIEVE TODAY

AFFIRMATIONS FOR THE DAY

MORNING

TODAY'S PERSONAL GOALS

PERSONALLY _____

RELATIONALLY_____

PROFESSIONALLY_____

NOTES:

TODAY I AM THANKFUL FOR...

1 _____

2 _____

3 _____

4 _____

5 _____

DEAR JOURNAL...

Journal Pages

How was your day? The highlights and how do you feel?

What does tomorrow look like for you? How can you make tomorrow a better day?

_____
_____
_____
_____
_____
_____
_____
_____
_____
_____
_____
_____
_____
_____
_____
_____
_____
_____
_____
_____
_____
_____

Date:
_____

ONE THING TO ACHIEVE TODAY

MORNING

AFFIRMATIONS FOR THE DAY

TODAY'S PERSONAL GOALS

☐ PERSONALLY _____

☐ RELATIONALLY_____

☐ PROFESSIONALLY_____

NOTES:

EVENING

TODAY I AM THANKFUL FOR...

1. _____
2. _____
3. _____
4. _____
5. _____

DEAR JOURNAL...

Journal Pages

How was your day? The highlights and how do you feel?

What does tomorrow look like for you? How can you make tomorrow a better day?

_____
_____
_____
_____
_____
_____
_____
_____
_____
_____
_____
_____
_____
_____
_____
_____
_____

Date:

ONE THING TO ACHIEVE TODAY

MORNING

AFFIRMATIONS FOR THE DAY

TODAY'S PERSONAL GOALS

PERSONALLY _____

RELATIONALLY _____

PROFESSIONALLY _____

NOTES:

EVENING

TODAY I AM THANKFUL FOR...

1. _____
2. _____
3. _____
4. _____
5. _____

DEAR JOURNAL...

Journal Pages

How was your day? The highlights and how do you feel?

What does tomorrow look like for you? How can you make tomorrow a better day?

_____
_____
_____
_____
_____
_____
_____
_____
_____
_____
_____
_____
_____
_____
_____
_____
_____
_____
_____

Date:

ONE THING TO ACHIEVE TODAY

MORNING

AFFIRMATIONS FOR THE DAY

TODAY'S PERSONAL GOALS

PERSONALLY _____

RELATIONALLY _____

PROFESSIONALLY _____

NOTES:

EVENING

1. _____
2. _____
3. _____
4. _____
5. _____

DEAR JOURNAL...

Journal Pages

How was your day? The highlights and how do you feel?
What does tomorrow look like for you? How can you make tomorrow a better day?

_____
_____
_____
_____
_____
_____
_____
_____
_____
_____
_____
_____
_____
_____
_____
_____
_____
_____

Journaling Page

Date:
_____

ONE THING TO ACHIEVE TODAY

AFFIRMATIONS FOR THE DAY

MORNING

TODAY'S PERSONAL GOALS

PERSONALLY _____

RELATIONALLY _____

PROFESSIONALLY _____

NOTES:

EVENING

TODAY I AM THANKFUL FOR...

1. _____
2. _____
3. _____
4. _____
5. _____

DEAR JOURNAL...

Journal Pages

How was your day? The highlights and how do you feel?

What does tomorrow look like for you? How can you make tomorrow a better day?

_____
_____
_____
_____
_____
_____
_____
_____
_____
_____
_____
_____
_____
_____
_____
_____
_____
_____

Date:

ONE THING TO ACHIEVE TODAY

AFFIRMATIONS FOR THE DAY

TODAY'S PERSONAL GOALS

MORNING

PERSONALLY _____

RELATIONALLY _____

PROFESSIONALLY _____

NOTES:

EVENING

TODAY I AM THANKFUL FOR...

1. _____
2. _____
3. _____
4. _____
5. _____

DEAR JOURNAL...

Journal Pages

How was your day? The highlights and how do you feel?

What does tomorrow look like for you? How can you make tomorrow a better day?

_____
_____
_____
_____
_____
_____
_____
_____
_____
_____
_____
_____
_____
_____
_____
_____
_____
_____
_____
_____

Date:
_____

ONE THING TO ACHIEVE TODAY

MORNING

AFFIRMATIONS FOR THE DAY

TODAY'S PERSONAL GOALS

PERSONALLY _____

RELATIONALLY _____

PROFESSIONALLY _____

NOTES:

EVENING

TODAY I AM THANKFUL FOR...

1. _____
2. _____
3. _____
4. _____
5. _____

DEAR JOURNAL...   *Journal Pages*

How was your day? The highlights and how do you feel?
What does tomorrow look like for you? How can you make tomorrow a better day?

_____
_____
_____
_____
_____
_____
_____
_____
_____
_____
_____
_____
_____
_____
_____
_____
_____
_____
_____

Journaling Pages

Date:

ONE THING TO ACHIEVE TODAY

MORNING

AFFIRMATIONS FOR THE DAY

TODAY'S PERSONAL GOALS

PERSONALLY _____

RELATIONALLY _____

PROFESSIONALLY _____

NOTES:

EVENING

TODAY I AM THANKFUL FOR...

1. _____
2. _____
3. _____
4. _____
5. _____

DEAR JOURNAL...

Journal Pages

How was your day? The highlights and how do you feel?

What does tomorrow look like for you? How can you make tomorrow a better day?

_____
_____
_____
_____
_____
_____
_____
_____
_____
_____
_____
_____
_____
_____
_____
_____
_____
_____
_____
_____

Date:
_____

ONE THING TO ACHIEVE TODAY

MORNING

AFFIRMATIONS FOR THE DAY

TODAY'S PERSONAL GOALS

☐ **PERSONALLY** _____

☐ **RELATIONALLY** _____

☐ **PROFESSIONALLY** _____

NOTES:

TODAY I AM THANKFUL FOR...

1 _____

2 _____

3 _____

4 _____

5 _____

DEAR JOURNAL...

Journal Pages

How was your day? The highlights and how do you feel?

What does tomorrow look like for you? How can you make tomorrow a better day?

_____
_____
_____
_____
_____
_____
_____
_____
_____
_____
_____
_____
_____
_____
_____
_____
_____
_____
_____

Journaling Page

Date:

ONE THING TO ACHIEVE TODAY

AFFIRMATIONS FOR THE DAY

MORNING

TODAY'S PERSONAL GOALS

PERSONALLY _____

RELATIONALLY _____

PROFESSIONALLY _____

NOTES:

EVENING

TODAY I AM THANKFUL FOR...

1. _____
2. _____
3. _____
4. _____
5. _____

DEAR JOURNAL...

Journal Pages

How was your day? The highlights and how do you feel?

What does tomorrow look like for you? How can you make tomorrow a better day?

_____
_____
_____
_____
_____
_____
_____
_____
_____
_____
_____
_____
_____
_____
_____
_____
_____
_____
_____
_____

Date:
_____

ONE THING TO ACHIEVE TODAY

AFFIRMATIONS FOR THE DAY

MORNING

TODAY'S PERSONAL GOALS

PERSONALLY _____

RELATIONALLY_____

PROFESSIONALLY_____

NOTES:

EVENING

TODAY I AM THANKFUL FOR...

1. _____
2. _____
3. _____
4. _____
5. _____

DEAR JOURNAL...

Journal Pages

How was your day? The highlights and how do you feel?

What does tomorrow look like for you? How can you make tomorrow a better day?

_____
_____
_____
_____
_____
_____
_____
_____
_____
_____
_____
_____
_____
_____
_____
_____
_____
_____
_____
_____
_____

Date:
_____

ONE THING TO ACHIEVE TODAY

MORNING

AFFIRMATIONS FOR THE DAY

TODAY'S PERSONAL GOALS

☐ **PERSONALLY** _____

☐ **RELATIONALLY** _____

☐ **PROFESSIONALLY** _____

NOTES:

EVENING

1. _____
2. _____
3. _____
4. _____
5. _____

DEAR JOURNAL... *Journal Pages*

How was your day? The highlights and how do you feel?
What does tomorrow look like for you? How can you make tomorrow a better day?

_____
_____
_____
_____
_____
_____
_____
_____
_____
_____
_____
_____
_____
_____
_____
_____
_____
_____
_____
_____

Date:
_____

ONE THING TO ACHIEVE TODAY

MORNING

AFFIRMATIONS FOR THE DAY

TODAY'S PERSONAL GOALS

☐ **PERSONALLY** _____

☐ **RELATIONALLY** _____

☐ **PROFESSIONALLY** _____

NOTES:

TODAY I AM THANKFUL FOR...

1 _____

2 _____

3 _____

4 _____

5 _____

DEAR JOURNAL...

Journal Pages

How was your day? The highlights and how do you feel?

What does tomorrow look like for you? How can you make tomorrow a better day?

_____
_____
_____
_____
_____
_____
_____
_____
_____
_____
_____
_____
_____
_____
_____
_____
_____
_____
_____
_____
_____

Journaling Pages

Date:
_____

ONE THING TO ACHIEVE TODAY

MORNING

AFFIRMATIONS FOR THE DAY

TODAY'S PERSONAL GOALS

☐ **PERSONALLY** _____

☐ **RELATIONALLY** _____

☐ **PROFESSIONALLY** _____

NOTES:

EVENING

TODAY I AM THANKFUL FOR...

1 _____
2 _____
3 _____
4 _____
5 _____

DEAR JOURNAL...

Journal Pages

How was your day? The highlights and how do you feel?
What does tomorrow look like for you? How can you make tomorrow a better day?

_____
_____
_____
_____
_____
_____
_____
_____
_____
_____
_____
_____
_____
_____
_____
_____
_____
_____
_____
_____
_____

Journaling Page

Journaling Pages

Date:

_____

ONE THING TO ACHIEVE TODAY

MORNING

AFFIRMATIONS FOR THE DAY

TODAY'S PERSONAL GOALS

☐ PERSONALLY _____

☐ RELATIONALLY _____

☐ PROFESSIONALLY _____

NOTES:

TODAY I AM THANKFUL FOR...

1 _____
2 _____
3 _____
4 _____
5 _____

DEAR JOURNAL...

Journal Pages

How was your day? The highlights and how do you feel?

What does tomorrow look like for you? How can you make tomorrow a better day?

_____
_____
_____
_____
_____
_____
_____
_____
_____
_____
_____
_____
_____
_____
_____
_____
_____
_____
_____
_____
_____
_____

Date:
_____

ONE THING TO ACHIEVE TODAY

MORNING

AFFIRMATIONS FOR THE DAY

TODAY'S PERSONAL GOALS

PERSONALLY _____

RELATIONALLY _____

PROFESSIONALLY _____

NOTES:

EVENING

1. _____
2. _____
3. _____
4. _____
5. _____

DEAR JOURNAL...

Journal Pages

How was your day? The highlights and how do you feel?

What does tomorrow look like for you? How can you make tomorrow a better day?

_____
_____
_____
_____
_____
_____
_____
_____
_____
_____
_____
_____
_____
_____
_____
_____
_____
_____
_____

Journaling Pages

Date: _____

ONE THING TO ACHIEVE TODAY

MORNING

AFFIRMATIONS FOR THE DAY

TODAY'S PERSONAL GOALS

PERSONALLY _____

RELATIONALLY_____

PROFESSIONALLY_____

NOTES:

EVENING

1. _____
2. _____
3. _____
4. _____
5. _____

DEAR JOURNAL...   *Journal Pages*

How was your day? The highlights and how do you feel?

What does tomorrow look like for you? How can you make tomorrow a better day?

_____
_____
_____
_____
_____
_____
_____
_____
_____
_____
_____
_____
_____
_____
_____
_____
_____
_____
_____
_____
_____

Journaling Pages

Date:
_____

ONE THING TO ACHIEVE TODAY

MORNING

AFFIRMATIONS FOR THE DAY

TODAY'S PERSONAL GOALS

PERSONALLY _____

RELATIONALLY _____

PROFESSIONALLY _____

NOTES:

EVENING

TODAY I AM THANKFUL FOR...

1. _____
2. _____
3. _____
4. _____
5. _____

DEAR JOURNAL...   *Journal Pages*

How was your day? The highlights and how do you feel?

What does tomorrow look like for you? How can you make tomorrow a better day?

_____
_____
_____
_____
_____
_____
_____
_____
_____
_____
_____
_____
_____
_____
_____
_____
_____
_____
_____
_____
_____

Journaling Pages

Date:
_____

ONE THING TO ACHIEVE TODAY

MORNING

AFFIRMATIONS FOR THE DAY

TODAY'S PERSONAL GOALS

PERSONALLY _____

RELATIONALLY _____

PROFESSIONALLY _____

NOTES:

EVENING

1 _____

2 _____

3 _____

4 _____

5 _____

DEAR JOURNAL...

Journal Pages

How was your day? The highlights and how do you feel?

What does tomorrow look like for you? How can you make tomorrow a better day?

_____
_____
_____
_____
_____
_____
_____
_____
_____
_____
_____
_____
_____
_____
_____
_____
_____
_____
_____
_____

Date:
_____

ONE THING TO ACHIEVE TODAY

MORNING

AFFIRMATIONS FOR THE DAY

TODAY'S PERSONAL GOALS

- **PERSONALLY** _____
- **RELATIONALLY** _____
- **PROFESSIONALLY** _____

NOTES:

EVENING

1 _____
2 _____
3 _____
4 _____
5 _____

DEAR JOURNAL... *Journal Pages*

How was your day? The highlights and how do you feel?

What does tomorrow look like for you? How can you make tomorrow a better day?

_____
_____
_____
_____
_____
_____
_____
_____
_____
_____
_____
_____
_____
_____
_____
_____
_____
_____
_____
_____

Date:

ONE THING TO ACHIEVE TODAY

MORNING

AFFIRMATIONS FOR THE DAY

TODAY'S PERSONAL GOALS

PERSONALLY _____

RELATIONALLY _____

PROFESSIONALLY _____

NOTES:

EVENING

1 _____
2 _____
3 _____
4 _____
5 _____

DEAR JOURNAL...   *Journal Pages*

How was your day? The highlights and how do you feel?
What does tomorrow look like for you? How can you make tomorrow a better day?

_____
_____
_____
_____
_____
_____
_____
_____
_____
_____
_____
_____
_____
_____
_____
_____
_____
_____
_____
_____
_____

Date:
_____

ONE THING TO ACHIEVE TODAY

MORNING

AFFIRMATIONS FOR THE DAY

TODAY'S PERSONAL GOALS

☐ **PERSONALLY** _____

☐ **RELATIONALLY** _____

☐ **PROFESSIONALLY** _____

NOTES:

EVENING

1 _____

2 _____

3 _____

4 _____

5 _____

DEAR JOURNAL...

Journal Pages

How was your day? The highlights and how do you feel?

What does tomorrow look like for you? How can you make tomorrow a better day?

_____
_____
_____
_____
_____
_____
_____
_____
_____
_____
_____
_____
_____
_____
_____
_____
_____
_____
_____
_____

Date:
_____

ONE THING TO ACHIEVE TODAY

MORNING

AFFIRMATIONS FOR THE DAY

TODAY'S PERSONAL GOALS

☐ **PERSONALLY** _____

☐ **RELATIONALLY** _____

☐ **PROFESSIONALLY** _____

NOTES:

EVENING

TODAY I AM THANKFUL FOR...

1 _____

2 _____

3 _____

4 _____

5 _____

DEAR JOURNAL...

Journal Pages

How was your day? The highlights and how do you feel?

What does tomorrow look like for you? How can you make tomorrow a better day?

_____
_____
_____
_____
_____
_____
_____
_____
_____
_____
_____
_____
_____
_____
_____
_____
_____
_____
_____
_____

Date:
_____

ONE THING TO ACHIEVE TODAY

MORNING

AFFIRMATIONS FOR THE DAY

TODAY'S PERSONAL GOALS

PERSONALLY _____

RELATIONALLY _____

PROFESSIONALLY _____

NOTES:

EVENING

TODAY I AM THANKFUL FOR...

1 _____

2 _____

3 _____

4 _____

5 _____

DEAR JOURNAL...

Journal Pages

How was your day? The highlights and how do you feel?

What does tomorrow look like for you? How can you make tomorrow a better day?

_____
_____
_____
_____
_____
_____
_____
_____
_____
_____
_____
_____
_____
_____
_____
_____
_____
_____
_____
_____

Journaling Page

Date:

ONE THING TO ACHIEVE TODAY

MORNING

AFFIRMATIONS FOR THE DAY

TODAY'S PERSONAL GOALS

PERSONALLY _____

RELATIONALLY _____

PROFESSIONALLY _____

NOTES:

EVENING

1 _____

2 _____

3 _____

4 _____

5 _____

DEAR JOURNAL...   *Journal Pages*

How was your day? The highlights and how do you feel?

What does tomorrow look like for you? How can you make tomorrow a better day?

_____
_____
_____
_____
_____
_____
_____
_____
_____
_____
_____
_____
_____
_____
_____
_____
_____
_____
_____
_____

Journaling Page

Date:

ONE THING TO ACHIEVE TODAY

MORNING

AFFIRMATIONS FOR THE DAY

TODAY'S PERSONAL GOALS

☐ **PERSONALLY** _____

☐ **RELATIONALLY** _____

☐ **PROFESSIONALLY** _____

NOTES:

EVENING

1 _____

2 _____

3 _____

4 _____

5 _____

DEAR JOURNAL...   *Journal Pages*

How was your day? The highlights and how do you feel?

What does tomorrow look like for you? How can you make tomorrow a better day?

_____
_____
_____
_____
_____
_____
_____
_____
_____
_____
_____
_____
_____
_____
_____
_____
_____
_____
_____
_____
_____

Date:
_____

ONE THING TO ACHIEVE TODAY

AFFIRMATIONS FOR THE DAY

TODAY'S PERSONAL GOALS

PERSONALLY _____

RELATIONALLY_____

PROFESSIONALLY_____

NOTES:

MORNING

EVENING

1. _____
2. _____
3. _____
4. _____
5. _____

DEAR JOURNAL...   *Journal Pages*

How was your day? The highlights and how do you feel?

What does tomorrow look like for you? How can you make tomorrow a better day?

_____
_____
_____
_____
_____
_____
_____
_____
_____
_____
_____
_____
_____
_____
_____
_____
_____
_____
_____
_____
_____

Date: _____

ONE THING TO ACHIEVE TODAY

MORNING

AFFIRMATIONS FOR THE DAY

TODAY'S PERSONAL GOALS

☐ PERSONALLY _____

☐ RELATIONALLY _____

☐ PROFESSIONALLY _____

NOTES:

EVENING

1 _____

2 _____

3 _____

4 _____

5 _____

DEAR JOURNAL... *Journal Pages*

How was your day? The highlights and how do you feel?

What does tomorrow look like for you? How can you make tomorrow a better day?

_____
_____
_____
_____
_____
_____
_____
_____
_____
_____
_____
_____
_____
_____
_____
_____
_____
_____
_____
_____
_____

Date: _____

ONE THING TO ACHIEVE TODAY

MORNING

AFFIRMATIONS FOR THE DAY

TODAY'S PERSONAL GOALS

☐ **PERSONALLY** _____

☐ **RELATIONALLY** _____

☐ **PROFESSIONALLY** _____

NOTES:

EVENING

1. _____
2. _____
3. _____
4. _____
5. _____

DEAR JOURNAL... *Journal Pages*

How was your day? The highlights and how do you feel?

What does tomorrow look like for you? How can you make tomorrow a better day?

_____
_____
_____
_____
_____
_____
_____
_____
_____
_____
_____
_____
_____
_____
_____
_____
_____
_____
_____
_____
_____
_____
_____

Date: _____

ONE THING TO ACHIEVE TODAY

AFFIRMATIONS FOR THE DAY

MORNING

TODAY'S PERSONAL GOALS

☐ **PERSONALLY** _____

☐ **RELATIONALLY** _____

☐ **PROFESSIONALLY** _____

NOTES:

EVENING

TODAY I AM THANKFUL FOR...

1 _____

2 _____

3 _____

4 _____

5 _____

DEAR JOURNAL...   *Journal Pages*

How was your day? The highlights and how do you feel?

What does tomorrow look like for you? How can you make tomorrow a better day?

_____
_____
_____
_____
_____
_____
_____
_____
_____
_____
_____
_____
_____
_____
_____
_____
_____
_____
_____
_____
_____

Date:
_____

ONE THING TO ACHIEVE TODAY

AFFIRMATIONS FOR THE DAY

MORNING

TODAY'S PERSONAL GOALS

☐ PERSONALLY _____

☐ RELATIONALLY _____

☐ PROFESSIONALLY _____

NOTES:

TODAY I AM THANKFUL FOR...

1 _____

2 _____

3 _____

4 _____

5 _____

DEAR JOURNAL...

Journal Pages

How was your day? The highlights and how do you feel?

What does tomorrow look like for you? How can you make tomorrow a better day?

_____
_____
_____
_____
_____
_____
_____
_____
_____
_____
_____
_____
_____
_____
_____
_____
_____
_____
_____
_____

Date:
_____

ONE THING TO ACHIEVE TODAY

MORNING

AFFIRMATIONS FOR THE DAY

TODAY'S PERSONAL GOALS

PERSONALLY _____

RELATIONALLY _____

PROFESSIONALLY _____

NOTES:

EVENING

TODAY I AM THANKFUL FOR...

1. _____
2. _____
3. _____
4. _____
5. _____

DEAR JOURNAL...   *Journal Pages*

How was your day? The highlights and how do you feel?
What does tomorrow look like for you? How can you make tomorrow a better day?

_____
_____
_____
_____
_____
_____
_____
_____
_____
_____
_____
_____
_____
_____
_____
_____
_____
_____
_____
_____
_____
_____

Date: _____

ONE THING TO ACHIEVE TODAY

MORNING

AFFIRMATIONS FOR THE DAY

TODAY'S PERSONAL GOALS

☐ **PERSONALLY** _____

☐ **RELATIONALLY** _____

☐ **PROFESSIONALLY** _____

NOTES:

EVENING

1. _____
2. _____
3. _____
4. _____
5. _____

DEAR JOURNAL...   *Journal Pages*

How was your day? The highlights and how do you feel?

What does tomorrow look like for you? How can you make tomorrow a better day?

_____
_____
_____
_____
_____
_____
_____
_____
_____
_____
_____
_____
_____
_____
_____
_____
_____
_____
_____
_____

Date:
_____

ONE THING TO ACHIEVE TODAY

AFFIRMATIONS FOR THE DAY

MORNING

TODAY'S PERSONAL GOALS

☐ **PERSONALLY** _____

☐ **RELATIONALLY** _____

☐ **PROFESSIONALLY** _____

NOTES:

TODAY I AM THANKFUL FOR...

1 _____

2 _____

3 _____

4 _____

5 _____

DEAR JOURNAL...

Journal Pages

How was your day? The highlights and how do you feel?

What does tomorrow look like for you? How can you make tomorrow a better day?

_____
_____
_____
_____
_____
_____
_____
_____
_____
_____
_____
_____
_____
_____
_____
_____
_____
_____
_____
_____

Date:
_____

ONE THING TO ACHIEVE TODAY

MORNING

AFFIRMATIONS FOR THE DAY

TODAY'S PERSONAL GOALS

PERSONALLY _____

RELATIONALLY _____

PROFESSIONALLY _____

NOTES:

EVENING

TODAY I AM THANKFUL FOR...

1. _____
2. _____
3. _____
4. _____
5. _____

DEAR JOURNAL...

Journal Pages

How was your day? The highlights and how do you feel?

What does tomorrow look like for you? How can you make tomorrow a better day?

_____
_____
_____
_____
_____
_____
_____
_____
_____
_____
_____
_____
_____
_____
_____
_____
_____
_____

Date:

ONE THING TO ACHIEVE TODAY

MORNING

AFFIRMATIONS FOR THE DAY

TODAY'S PERSONAL GOALS

PERSONALLY _____

RELATIONALLY_____

PROFESSIONALLY_____

NOTES:

EVENING

1 _____
2 _____
3 _____
4 _____
5 _____

DEAR JOURNAL...

Journal Pages

How was your day? The highlights and how do you feel?

What does tomorrow look like for you? How can you make tomorrow a better day?

_____
_____
_____
_____
_____
_____
_____
_____
_____
_____
_____
_____
_____
_____
_____
_____
_____
_____
_____
_____
_____

Date:
_____

ONE THING TO ACHIEVE TODAY

MORNING

AFFIRMATIONS FOR THE DAY

TODAY'S PERSONAL GOALS

☐ **PERSONALLY** _____

☐ **RELATIONALLY** _____

☐ **PROFESSIONALLY** _____

NOTES:

EVENING

1. _____
2. _____
3. _____
4. _____
5. _____

DEAR JOURNAL...

Journal Pages

How was your day? The highlights and how do you feel?

What does tomorrow look like for you? How can you make tomorrow a better day?

_____
_____
_____
_____
_____
_____
_____
_____
_____
_____
_____
_____
_____
_____
_____
_____
_____
_____
_____
_____

Date: _____

ONE THING TO ACHIEVE TODAY

MORNING

AFFIRMATIONS FOR THE DAY

TODAY'S PERSONAL GOALS

PERSONALLY _____

RELATIONALLY _____

PROFESSIONALLY _____

NOTES:

EVENING

TODAY I AM THANKFUL FOR...

1. _____
2. _____
3. _____
4. _____
5. _____

DEAR JOURNAL...

Journal Pages

How was your day? The highlights and how do you feel?

What does tomorrow look like for you? How can you make tomorrow a better day?

_____
_____
_____
_____
_____
_____
_____
_____
_____
_____
_____
_____
_____
_____
_____
_____
_____
_____
_____
_____

Journaling Page

Journaling Pages

Date: _____

ONE THING TO ACHIEVE TODAY

AFFIRMATIONS FOR THE DAY

MORNING

TODAY'S PERSONAL GOALS

☐ **PERSONALLY** _____

☐ **RELATIONALLY** _____

☐ **PROFESSIONALLY** _____

NOTES:

EVENING

TODAY I AM THANKFUL FOR...

1 _____

2 _____

3 _____

4 _____

5 _____

DEAR JOURNAL...   *Journal Pages*

How was your day? The highlights and how do you feel?

What does tomorrow look like for you? How can you make tomorrow a better day?

_____
_____
_____
_____
_____
_____
_____
_____
_____
_____
_____
_____
_____
_____
_____
_____
_____
_____
_____

Date:
_____

ONE THING TO ACHIEVE TODAY

AFFIRMATIONS FOR THE DAY

MORNING

TODAY'S PERSONAL GOALS

PERSONALLY _____

RELATIONALLY_____

PROFESSIONALLY_____

NOTES:

EVENING

1 _____

2 _____

3 _____

4 _____

5 _____

DEAR JOURNAL...   *Journal Pages*

How was your day? The highlights and how do you feel?

What does tomorrow look like for you? How can you make tomorrow a better day?

_____
_____
_____
_____
_____
_____
_____
_____
_____
_____
_____
_____
_____
_____
_____
_____
_____
_____

Date:
_____

ONE THING TO ACHIEVE TODAY

MORNING

AFFIRMATIONS FOR THE DAY

TODAY'S PERSONAL GOALS

☐ **PERSONALLY** _____

☐ **RELATIONALLY**_____

☐ **PROFESSIONALLY**_____

NOTES:

EVENING

1. _____
2. _____
3. _____
4. _____
5. _____

DEAR JOURNAL...   *Journal Pages*

How was your day? The highlights and how do you feel?

What does tomorrow look like for you? How can you make tomorrow a better day?

_____
_____
_____
_____
_____
_____
_____
_____
_____
_____
_____
_____
_____
_____
_____
_____
_____
_____
_____
_____
_____

Journaling Page

Journaling Pages

Date:
_____

ONE THING TO ACHIEVE TODAY

AFFIRMATIONS FOR THE DAY

MORNING

TODAY'S PERSONAL GOALS

☐ **PERSONALLY** _____

☐ **RELATIONALLY** _____

☐ **PROFESSIONALLY** _____

NOTES:

EVENING

1. _____
2. _____
3. _____
4. _____
5. _____

DEAR JOURNAL...

Journal Pages

How was your day? The highlights and how do you feel?

What does tomorrow look like for you? How can you make tomorrow a better day?

_____
_____
_____
_____
_____
_____
_____
_____
_____
_____
_____
_____
_____
_____
_____
_____
_____
_____
_____

Date:
_____

ONE THING TO ACHIEVE TODAY

AFFIRMATIONS FOR THE DAY

MORNING

TODAY'S PERSONAL GOALS

■ **PERSONALLY** _____

■ **RELATIONALLY** _____

■ **PROFESSIONALLY** _____

NOTES:

EVENING

1. _____
2. _____
3. _____
4. _____
5. _____

DEAR JOURNAL... *Journal Pages*

How was your day? The highlights and how do you feel?
What does tomorrow look like for you? How can you make tomorrow a better day?

_____
_____
_____
_____
_____
_____
_____
_____
_____
_____
_____
_____
_____
_____
_____
_____
_____
_____
_____
_____
_____
_____

Date:
_____

ONE THING TO ACHIEVE TODAY

MORNING

AFFIRMATIONS FOR THE DAY

TODAY'S PERSONAL GOALS

PERSONALLY _____

RELATIONALLY _____

PROFESSIONALLY _____

NOTES:

EVENING

TODAY I AM THANKFUL FOR...

1 _____

2 _____

3 _____

4 _____

5 _____

DEAR JOURNAL...

Journal Pages

How was your day? The highlights and how do you feel?

What does tomorrow look like for you? How can you make tomorrow a better day?

_____
_____
_____
_____
_____
_____
_____
_____
_____
_____
_____
_____
_____
_____
_____
_____
_____
_____
_____

Date:
_____

ONE THING TO ACHIEVE TODAY

AFFIRMATIONS FOR THE DAY

MORNING

TODAY'S PERSONAL GOALS

PERSONALLY _____

RELATIONALLY _____

PROFESSIONALLY _____

NOTES:

EVENING

TODAY I AM THANKFUL FOR...

1. _____
2. _____
3. _____
4. _____
5. _____

DEAR JOURNAL...

Journal Pages

How was your day? The highlights and how do you feel?

What does tomorrow look like for you? How can you make tomorrow a better day?

_____
_____
_____
_____
_____
_____
_____
_____
_____
_____
_____
_____
_____
_____
_____
_____
_____
_____
_____
_____
_____

Date:

ONE THING TO ACHIEVE TODAY

MORNING

AFFIRMATIONS FOR THE DAY

TODAY'S PERSONAL GOALS

PERSONALLY _____

RELATIONALLY _____

PROFESSIONALLY _____

NOTES:

EVENING

TODAY I AM THANKFUL FOR...

1. _____
2. _____
3. _____
4. _____
5. _____

DEAR JOURNAL...   *Journal Pages*

How was your day? The highlights and how do you feel?
What does tomorrow look like for you? How can you make tomorrow a better day?

_____
_____
_____
_____
_____
_____
_____
_____
_____
_____
_____
_____
_____
_____
_____
_____
_____
_____

Date: _____

ONE THING TO ACHIEVE TODAY

MORNING

AFFIRMATIONS FOR THE DAY

TODAY'S PERSONAL GOALS

- **PERSONALLY** _____
- **RELATIONALLY** _____
- **PROFESSIONALLY** _____

NOTES:

EVENING

1 _____

2 _____

3 _____

4 _____

5 _____

DEAR JOURNAL...

Journal Pages

How was your day? The highlights and how do you feel?

What does tomorrow look like for you? How can you make tomorrow a better day?

_____
_____
_____
_____
_____
_____
_____
_____
_____
_____
_____
_____
_____
_____
_____
_____
_____
_____

Date:
_____

ONE THING TO ACHIEVE TODAY

AFFIRMATIONS FOR THE DAY

MORNING

TODAY'S PERSONAL GOALS

PERSONALLY _____

RELATIONALLY _____

PROFESSIONALLY _____

NOTES:

EVENING

1. _____
2. _____
3. _____
4. _____
5. _____

DEAR JOURNAL...   *Journal Pages*

How was your day? The highlights and how do you feel?

What does tomorrow look like for you? How can you make tomorrow a better day?

_____
_____
_____
_____
_____
_____
_____
_____
_____
_____
_____
_____
_____
_____
_____
_____
_____
_____
_____
_____
_____

Journaling Page

Date:
_____

ONE THING TO ACHIEVE TODAY

AFFIRMATIONS FOR THE DAY

TODAY'S PERSONAL GOALS

MORNING

☐ PERSONALLY _____

☐ RELATIONALLY_____

☐ PROFESSIONALLY_____

NOTES:

EVENING

TODAY I AM THANKFUL FOR...

1
2
3
4
5

DEAR JOURNAL...   *Journal Pages*

How was your day? The highlights and how do you feel?

What does tomorrow look like for you? How can you make tomorrow a better day?

Date:

ONE THING TO ACHIEVE TODAY

MORNING

AFFIRMATIONS FOR THE DAY

TODAY'S PERSONAL GOALS

PERSONALLY _____

RELATIONALLY _____

PROFESSIONALLY _____

NOTES:

EVENING

TODAY I AM THANKFUL FOR...

1. _____
2. _____
3. _____
4. _____
5. _____

DEAR JOURNAL...   *Journal Pages*

How was your day? The highlights and how do you feel?

What does tomorrow look like for you? How can you make tomorrow a better day?

_____
_____
_____
_____
_____
_____
_____
_____
_____
_____
_____
_____
_____
_____
_____
_____
_____
_____
_____
_____

Journaling Pages

Date: _____

ONE THING TO ACHIEVE TODAY

MORNING

AFFIRMATIONS FOR THE DAY

TODAY'S PERSONAL GOALS

☐ **PERSONALLY** _____

☐ **RELATIONALLY** _____

☐ **PROFESSIONALLY** _____

NOTES:

EVENING

1. _____
2. _____
3. _____
4. _____
5. _____

DEAR JOURNAL... *Journal Pages*

How was your day? The highlights and how do you feel?
What does tomorrow look like for you? How can you make tomorrow a better day?

_____
_____
_____
_____
_____
_____
_____
_____
_____
_____
_____
_____
_____
_____
_____
_____
_____
_____
_____

Date:
_____

ONE THING TO ACHIEVE TODAY

MORNING

AFFIRMATIONS FOR THE DAY

TODAY'S PERSONAL GOALS

☐ PERSONALLY _____

☐ RELATIONALLY _____

☐ PROFESSIONALLY _____

NOTES:

EVENING

TODAY I AM THANKFUL FOR...

1 _____

2 _____

3 _____

4 _____

5 _____

DEAR JOURNAL...   *Journal Pages*

How was your day? The highlights and how do you feel?

What does tomorrow look like for you? How can you make tomorrow a better day?

_____
_____
_____
_____
_____
_____
_____
_____
_____
_____
_____
_____
_____
_____
_____
_____
_____
_____
_____

Date:
_____

ONE THING TO ACHIEVE TODAY

AFFIRMATIONS FOR THE DAY

MORNING

TODAY'S PERSONAL GOALS

☐ PERSONALLY _____

☐ RELATIONALLY _____

☐ PROFESSIONALLY _____

NOTES:

EVENING

TODAY I AM THANKFUL FOR...

1. _____
2. _____
3. _____
4. _____
5. _____

DEAR JOURNAL...   *Journal Pages*

How was your day? The highlights and how do you feel?

What does tomorrow look like for you? How can you make tomorrow a better day?

_____
_____
_____
_____
_____
_____
_____
_____
_____
_____
_____
_____
_____
_____
_____
_____
_____
_____
_____

Journaling Page

Journaling Pages

Date:
_____

ONE THING TO ACHIEVE TODAY

MORNING

AFFIRMATIONS FOR THE DAY

TODAY'S PERSONAL GOALS

☐ **PERSONALLY** _____

☐ **RELATIONALLY** _____

☐ **PROFESSIONALLY** _____

NOTES:

EVENING

TODAY I AM THANKFUL FOR...

1. _____
2. _____
3. _____
4. _____
5. _____

DEAR JOURNAL...

Journal Pages

How was your day? The highlights and how do you feel?

What does tomorrow look like for you? How can you make tomorrow a better day?

_____
_____
_____
_____
_____
_____
_____
_____
_____
_____
_____
_____
_____
_____
_____
_____
_____
_____
_____

Date:
_____

ONE THING TO ACHIEVE TODAY

MORNING

AFFIRMATIONS FOR THE DAY

TODAY'S PERSONAL GOALS

☐ **PERSONALLY** _____

☐ **RELATIONALLY** _____

☐ **PROFESSIONALLY** _____

NOTES:

EVENING

1. _____
2. _____
3. _____
4. _____
5. _____

DEAR JOURNAL...   *Journal Pages*

How was your day? The highlights and how do you feel?

What does tomorrow look like for you? How can you make tomorrow a better day?

_____
_____
_____
_____
_____
_____
_____
_____
_____
_____
_____
_____
_____
_____
_____
_____
_____
_____
_____
_____
_____